USBORNE
WRITE YOUR OWN
SCRIPTS

USBORNE
WRITE YOUR OWN
SCRIPTS

With scripts written by...

Faith   McErlaine

Contents

These are quick tips and tricks to get you started.

Writing scripts

Write a scary script.

You can write your own scripts in this section.

learn all about audio drama.

Next steps

How to turn a script into a show.

Usborne Quicklinks

For links to websites where you can find more tips and inspiration for writing your own exciting scripts, go to **usborne.com/Quicklinks** and enter the keywords **write your own scripts**. You can also download some of the planning pages from this book to help you write more scripts and turn them into shows.

Please follow the online safety guidelines at Usborne Quicklinks. Children should be supervised online.

What is a script?

There's more than one way to tell a story. You can say it out loud. You can write it down for someone to read. Or you can write it as a script for people to perform in front of an audience.

A story book is a little like a one-way conversation between an author and a reader. But a script isn't a finished piece of work like a story book. It's an instruction manual that tells performers and other readers HOW to tell your story.

Here are some things your script should include...

Where your story takes place
– the SETTING

What your characters SAY – the DIALOGUE

What your characters DO – the ACTION

Then arise my friend, and let our adventure begin...

Who is in the story and what they look like – the CAST

Any objects that performers might pick up, or use – the PROPS

Scripts look different from other forms of writing. All the information is separated out so it's clear what needs to be done – and when. That's because a script isn't really meant to be read – it's meant to be PERFORMED.

Scripts are usually broken down into different SCENES.

The name of the CHARACTER speaking comes before the dialogue, to make it clear who is saying what.

A script should contain all the information someone else would need to tell the story. It can also suggest certain SPECIAL EFFECTS, such as lighting.

The SETTING is described before the dialogue and the action. This helps people design the set.

Performers are told where they should be at the start of the scene and when they should ENTER.

ACTIONS and DIALOGUE are written on separate lines.

SCENE 1

The curtain rises to reveal a palm-fringed beach. QUEEN AURORA stands majestically at the front of the stage.

LITTLE JIM enters, dragging a treasure chest behind him. He flings open the chest.

QUEEN AURORA: You never fail me, Little Jim. I see you've found the Captain's gold.

LITTLE JIM: I live to serve, Your Highness.

QUEEN AURORA: And I depend on your help. But there is one more thing we must do before we can save the Sea King and his people. Will you join me?

LITTLE JIM kneels down.

LITTLE JIM: I will.

LITTLE JIM is suddenly bathed in a golden light that shines down from above.

QUEEN AURORA: Then arise my friend, and let our adventure begin...

Telling a story

There's one thing all the best scripts have in common – a great story. Before you start writing anything, you need to decide what sort of story you want to tell.

You can write a script for absolutely ANY type of story you want.

A script can be...

Futuristic

Happy

Surprising

Exciting

Romantic

Scary

Mysterious

Sad

Funny

You don't even have to come up with a new story yourself. You could RETELL one you already know.

Magical

Silly

Historical

Write the titles of three stories you'd like to retell here.

1. ....

2. ....

3. ....

Like every story, a script needs a BEGINNING, a MIDDLE and an END. This will make your story more satisfying for your audience. You can follow a structure like this, to keep on track as you write.

Beginning
Introduce a character who has a problem.

Middle
Your character tries to solve the problem.

The problem becomes more complicated.

End
Your character solves the problem.

Once you have a story idea, you can decide what sort of script you want to write...

It could be a play...

...a movie...

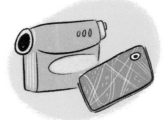

...or an audio drama.

The Earth looks so beautiful from space!

Live drama is exciting, but performers can make mistakes, so it's best to keep the action and dialogue simple.

You don't need special equipment to make your own movie – you can do it with a phone or a digital camera.

Audio dramas don't include anything visual at all, so they leave lots of room for your audience to imagine things.

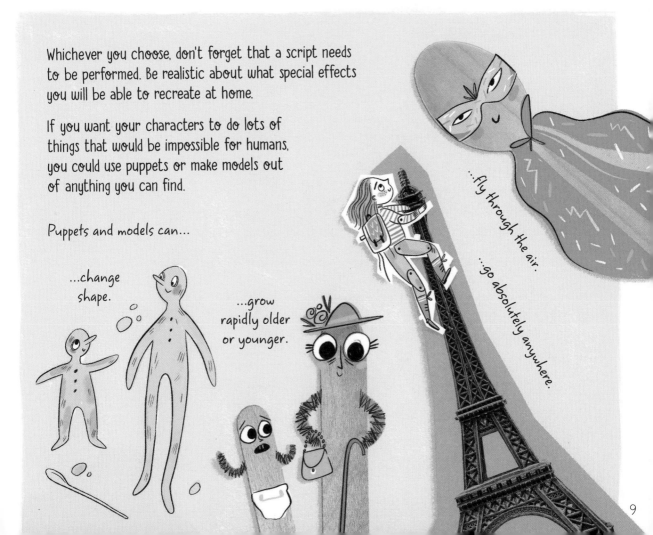

Whichever you choose, don't forget that a script needs to be performed. Be realistic about what special effects you will be able to recreate at home.

If you want your characters to do lots of things that would be impossible for humans, you could use puppets or make models out of anything you can find.

Puppets and models can...

...change shape.

...grow rapidly older or younger.

...fly through the air.

...go absolutely anywhere.

Start with characters

If you're not writing a script based on an existing story, a good place to start is to invent your main character.

1. Start with a simple idea for a character – a super genius, for example.

2. Give your character a goal – some way she wants to change her life.

3. Now create a source of conflict – something that stands in the way of what your character wants.

Make up different characters of your own below. Then build their stories around them.

Character	Goal	Conflict
Marrissa hay wood	To go to collage in NY	My enemy is failing me on purpose

"Will the hero fall in love?"

"Will the hero learn a lesson?"

"Will the hero escape?"

4. Who is behind this conflict? This person will be your main character's opponent.

A mathematics professor

5. Think about a setting where your main character and opponent might meet.

A college

6. Every script should revolve around a BIG QUESTION that concerns your main character.

Should a robot be allowed to study with humans?

Opponent	Setting	Big question
Lexi Conwall	High School (Hamilton)	What will my future be like if I get into Collage?

You can turn these characters' stories into scripts later in this book.

Bringing characters to life

Your characters are the beating heart of your story. So how do you make up a good one? One way is to answer a few questions.

Pick one of the characters you created on the previous page and answer this questionnaire about them. Not all the details you invent will come up in your script, but your answers will help you understand what makes your character tick.

Name: Marrissa haywood

Age: 16   Gender: Female

Goal: To get to collage in NY

Conflict: Lexi fails my grades on purpouse by changing my grades online from A's & B's — E'sAF's

Where does your character live? Widnes

Who does your character live with? Mum, dad & older sister

What does your character do every day? Puts make-up & Straightens hair.

What three words best describe your character's personality?
Idependent, brave, kind

What does your character look like?
Short ginger hair, freckles and a nice smily mouth

How does your character dress?
Casually but fashionable

What's a typical gesture for your character?

Gestures

Scripts show characters' personalities through actions, so it's really useful to think of a character's typical gestures. A shy person might hide behind a hat. An angry person might break things.

Loves? Family, Sewing, Sleeping, Food, Friends, Art

Hates?

bullies, show offs, Languages, ppl looking through privacy.

Best qualities?

bright, bubbly :), Pretty

Worst flaws?

always hungry

Best friend?

Zara dunkin :) Finlay hill :) Hannah harper :) Mollie marsden :) Poppie

Biggest enemy?

Lexi Conwall :C

Deepest secret?

Has a crush on Finlay

Biggest fears?

Spiders, rats

How do your character's flaws, secrets and fears create problems?

What kind of animal is your character most like, and why?

Seal bc seals r always looking for adventures - like Marrissa.

What is your character's earliest memory?

It's a good idea to answer questions like these for all the important characters in your scripts.

Writing dialogue

In a script, dialogue is more than just a conversation – it moves the story along and helps make the characters feel real. Here are three tips for writing good dialogue.

1. Don't be too obvious

Dialogue sounds more natural if it gives small hints about what a character is feeling, or what is going on rather than spelling out everything exactly.

2. Be messy

Most people don't talk in perfect sentences. They use slang and contractions – "I'm" instead of "I am" or "don't" instead of "do not" – and they say "um" a lot. Read your dialogue aloud as you write to make sure it sounds natural.

3. Keep it moving

Try to keep your speeches short. Real conversation usually bounces back and forth like a tennis match. A good rule is that you shouldn't give a character more than three lines of dialogue at a time.

HANSEL

Father has left us alone in the forest. That must mean he doesn't love us.

HANSEL

I don't think father's coming back.

GRETEL

I do not think it is a good idea for you to eat that, Hansel.

GRETEL

Um... that's a super bad idea, Hansel.

You never listen to me!

Try some. It tastes like peppermint!

Sooo... did somebody knock?

Speech safari

Now it's time to be a spy. You can get a feel for how people talk by listening to conversations going on around you. Write down snippets of good or interesting dialogue in the speech bubbles. Later, you might be able to include them in your own scripts.

Listen out for...

- repeated phrases
- popular slang
- different ways of saying "yes"
- noises people make instead of words

Dialogue reveals your characters' emotions and personalities. You can completely change their moods by changing their dialogue.

One lollipop please.

Neutral

You better give me that! NOW!

Angry

Do you think I might possibly buy, um, a-a lollipop?

Hesitant

It's not air that keeps it floating, dummy — it's helium.

Cocky

This is the most awesome birthday ever!

Enthusiastic

What would it be like to be a balloon?

Dreamy

Moods and attitudes

angry, anxious, bossy, brave, clueless, confident, cruel, curious, delighted, desperate, disappointed, encouraging, foolish, fun, helpful, hopeful, jealous, jokey, loving, passionate, relaxed, sad, sassy, scared, secretive, snobby, stubborn, suspicious, whiny

Fill in the speech bubbles below, showing a different emotion or attitude each time.
You could pick a mood from the list opposite, or choose your own.
Which version works best for you?

Mood: ....

Mood: ....

Mood: ....

Mood: ....

Mood: ....

Mood: ....

For the story below pick two **contrasting** moods for the two characters and then write their conversation in the speech bubbles.

Mood: ....

Mood: ....

Mood:

Mood:

Now pick two new and completely **different** moods for the characters and write a new conversation for the same scene. The more your characters' moods clash, the more interesting your dialogue will be.

Giving instructions

Writing dialogue is important, but a script should also include instructions so readers know what's going on, and performers know what to do.

Dialogue on its own doesn't tell the whole story, as this short scene shows.

> GIRL: What's going on here?
> BOY: Err...
> GIRL: Caught in the ACT!

Adding some details will make things clearer. Here you can see how adding different details changes the dialogue above into four very different scenes.

You can suggest a particular **setting** for the scene.

> BOY stands in a messy kitchen, surrounded by crumbs and empty cookie jars.
>   GIRL: What's going on here?
>   BOY: Err...
>   GIRL: Caught in the ACT!

Or you could suggest **costumes** for characters to wear.

> GIRL wears a police hat. BOY wears a striped top and black mask.
>   GIRL: What's going on here?
>   BOY: Err...
>   GIRL: Caught in the ACT!

You might suggest **actions** for characters to perform.

> BOY is asleep at a desk, surrounded by school books. He snores.
>   GIRL: What's going on here?
> GIRL taps BOY on the arm. He wakes up.
>   BOY: Err...
>   GIRL: Caught in the ACT!

You can even suggest **props** for characters to use, too.

> BOY is painting a picture. He tries to hide it from GIRL, but she sees.
>   GIRL: What's going on here?
> GIRL holds up the picture — it's her face surrounded by hearts.
>   BOY: Err...
>   GIRL: Caught in the ACT!

Try adding your own instructions to the short scenes below. Remember to keep your suggestions BRIEF and RELEVANT – there's no point suggesting a character wears a rabbit costume if it doesn't add anything to your story.

Setting:

Costume:

GIRL: Can I help you?

BOY: I hope so...

> You can add **actions** and **props** between the lines of dialogue.

Setting:

Costume:

GIRL: You'll never believe the day I've had.

BOY: Is that what I think it is?

Setting:

Costume:

GIRL: I'm afraid I've got some bad news.

BOY: Well, so have I...

First impressions

The first time you introduce a character it's a good idea to include a few well-chosen details. This helps anyone reading your script – actors, readers or directors – to understand the character.

This introduction of a pirate captain is very plain.

> On the ship, CAPTAIN BOB looks through a telescope at the sea.

But *this* description gives more clues about what Captain Bob is like.

> Poised, chest puffed out, at the top of the mast, CAPTAIN BOB scans the horizon through a telescope. Bob's long hair flows in the wind. Bob's hand is trembling.

This tells us Captain Bob is VAIN and likes to pose heroically. Bob's also SCARED OF HEIGHTS.

How would you describe Captain Bob in these different situations...

...climbing down to the deck?

...swimming?

...eating a sandwich?

...getting ready for bed?

Now try writing introductions for other members of Captain Bob's pirate crew.
Think of things each character could be doing to reveal their personalities.

Name / job	Personality	Description of character in action
Roderick – the ship's cook	lazy	
Jenny – the navigator	nervous	
Dita – the first mate	reckless	
Ezekiel – the lookout	extremely careful	
Pansy – the ship's monkey	crafty	

Adding the right details

Descriptions in scripts set the scene and describe the action. They should be short and to the point, so make sure to choose the right details.

Here's an image of a short scene and a description of that scene as it might be written in a script.

Layla frantically searches the meadow for a spider daisy. There are lots of flowers. She doesn't notice the robot bee buzzing closer as she crawls across the grass. A relieved smile flashes across her face when she finds the flower at last. Poison glistens on the bee's stinger. It flies closer.

Here are five top tips for writing descriptions:

1. Write in the present tense

Writing in the present tense makes descriptions feel lively.

2. Leave out a lot

You don't need to include everything – just keep the key details that tell your story.

3. Only describe what you can see

Give your characters actions that show the audience what they are thinking and feeling. Don't *say* a character is cold, describe that character shivering to *show* that he or she is cold.

5. Think of images

When you are trying to describe a complicated action sequence, such as a fight or a race, it helps to break down the action into a series of images like in a comic book.

4. Use vivid words

Every word needs to count, so make sure you use the right ones. How, exactly, does your character read a book? Does your character doze off, or flick through, or devour it?

Now write a brief description for each of these scenes.

The outline of a script

Scripts are often divided into short sections called scenes. A scene describes what happens in one location at one time. When you want to change the time or the location, you start a new scene.

Here is an outline of Little Red Riding Hood, broken down into scenes to show you how they work.

SCENE 1: NICE COTTAGE, MORNING
Little Red's mother gives her cake for Grandmother. "Don't talk to strangers."

Headings say where the scene takes place and at what time of day.

SCENE 2: THE FOREST, MORNING
Little Red picks flowers. She tells a hungry wolf where she is going.

Scenes can jump forward in time. It's a good trick to miss out the boring parts.

SCENE 3: GRANDMOTHER'S COTTAGE, MORNING
The wolf pretends to be Little Red, then gobbles up Grandmother.

SCENE 4: GRANDMOTHER'S COTTAGE, MORNING
Little Red arrives. The wolf pretends to be Grandmother, then gobbles her up.

SCENE 5: FOREST, AFTERNOON
Outside, a woodcutter hears the wolf snoring.

SCENE 6: GRANDMOTHER'S COTTAGE, AFTERNOON
The woodcutter runs in and cuts open the wolf's belly. Little Red and Grandmother jump out.

finishing a scene before you explain what is going on is a good way to set up a mystery.

SCENE 7: FOREST, AFTERNOON
Little Red gathers stones.

Scenes can be very short.

SCENE 8: GRANDMOTHER'S COTTAGE, AFTERNOON
Grandmother puts the stones into the wolf's belly and sews it shut.

SCENE 9: THE FOREST, SUNSET
The wolf wakes up with the stones rumbling in his belly. He cannot sneak up on anyone ever again. He watches Little Red go home.

The mystery of what the stones are for is explained.

Take a fairy tale or another story you like and use this space to write a scene-by-scene outline for it.

SCENE 1:

Scene length

Think about what kind of show you want to make. A script for a film can have lots of short scenes. Plays usually have fewer scenes as changing scenery can be hard when you perform on a stage.

WRITING SCRIPTS

In the next section you will have an opportunity to write scripts for different scenes. As you go, try to use some of the tips and tricks you've already learned.

Before you start

Here's a handy checklist of things you might think about as you plan each scene. Write out your ideas on a piece of scrap paper.

1. List the characters in the scene.

2. Write down what each character wants to achieve in the scene.

3. Make sure your characters have distinct voices so you can tell them apart.

4. Decide where the scene is set.

5. Identify at least one interesting detail about the setting. How might you use it?

From story to script

Writing a script is like writing any story – the information is just presented differently.

Below is how part of *Goldilocks and the Three Bears* might be written in a story book.

The three bears let themselves into the cottage. They felt tired and hungry after their walk. As they looked around the room, Father Bear thought something felt wrong. He started to worry. Then, he noticed something that made him very cross.

"Someone's been sitting in my chair," he said.

"And someone's been sitting in my chair," added Mother Bear.

"Well someone's been sitting in MY chair," said Baby Bear, suddenly feeling very upset. "And now it's BROKEN!"

"Don't worry, we can fix it later, darling," Mother Bear said. "First, we should check the house. Whoever it is might still be here." And, with that, the three bears marched into the next room to see if anyone was there.

Story books are often written in the past tense because they're describing something that has already happened.

A story book writer can go INSIDE characters' heads and tell readers what they're thinking and feeling.

This is how the same part of the story might be written if it was a script, instead.

A script is written in the present tense because the story unfolds as the performers act it out.

A red front door opens directly onto a room in a cottage. On the other side of the room, there is a brown door. In the middle of the stage, there are three chairs of different sizes. The smallest one is broken.

FATHER BEAR, MOTHER BEAR and BABY BEAR enter through the front door.

FATHER BEAR sniffs the air. He looks confused and frowns. He stamps over to the biggest chair. He bends down and sniffs it.

    FATHER BEAR: Someone's been sitting in my chair.

MOTHER BEAR walks to the medium-sized chair. She sniffs it too.

    MOTHER BEAR: And someone's been sitting in my chair.

BABY BEAR points at the smallest chair and starts to cry.

    BABY BEAR: Well someone's been sitting in MY chair. And now it's BROKEN!

    MOTHER BEAR: Don't worry, we can fix it later, darling. First, we should check the house. Whoever it is might still be here.

MOTHER BEAR, FATHER BEAR and BABY BEAR exit through the brown door.

The setting is described first.

Performers are told when and where they should be at the start of the scene.

The dialogue doesn't need to change. It's exactly the same as it was in the story book.

Actions can be used to show what the characters are thinking or feeling.

Performers are told when and where they should be at the end of the scene.

Turn the page to continue...

This is how the story book continues.

The three bears rushed into their kitchen. At first glance everything looked just as they had left it. The cupboards were still stocked with plenty of honey and their bowls of porridge were still laid out on the table. Then Father Bear looked more closely. He wasn't happy. He picked up his spoon and put it down.

"Someone's been eating my porridge," he said. Mother Bear inspected her bowl, too. "And someone's been eating my porridge," she said.

"Well, someone's been eating my porridge," said Baby Bear, pointing to his empty bowl. "And they've gobbled it all up!"

Baby Bear was too angry to be upset now.

"Let's take a look upstairs," Mother Bear said. Father Bear and Baby Bear followed her out of the room.

How would you write this part of the story as a script? Here are some tips to help you...

Think about the SETTING – where this part of the story is taking place and what it looks like.

Remember to write down the NAMES of all the characters as they ENTER and EXIT.

Look out for any PROPS or FURNITURE your script should mention. Circle these in the story above.

Think about what the characters are DOING. Draw boxes around any doing words so you can include them in your instructions.

Underline all the DIALOGUE so you can copy it out at the right point in the script.

What are the characters THINKING or FEELING? Try to imagine how your performers might SHOW this – either with their facial expressions or their actions.

Now use this page to rewrite the story opposite as a script.

ction sequences are thrilling scenes such as chases, fights and escapes.
nlike most scenes in a script, action sequences don't involve a lot of
ialogue. Instead, they mostly describe what your characters are doing.

All is quiet...

Uh oh...

Oh no!

Instead of dialogue,
show how your
haracter feels through
actions: cowering in
fear, for example.

Eeek!

AAARGHHH!

Here is an outline to help you plan an action sequence.

All is quiet...

Give your characters a quiet moment before the action kicks off.

Uh oh...

A surprise happens that gets the action started. Your hero is now in danger.

Oh no!

Things get worse. Don't slow down. Keep adding exciting twists to the scene.

Eeek!

Your characters face a difficult decision. Their choices reveal their personalities, strengths and weaknesses.

AAARGHHH!

Keep your most exciting and dangerous moment for the end. That way your scene will feel more dramatic.

Example

At home, Sunil watches TV with his dog Baxter. Behind them, a shadow creeps closer.

A skeleton jumps out and grabs Sunil. Baxter bites the skeleton. Sunil breaks free and runs downstairs.

There is another skeleton downstairs! Sunil hides in a dark room, but Baxter is cornered.

Watching from his hiding place, Sunil is terrified. Should he stay hidden or try to save Baxter?

Summoning all his courage, Sunil bursts out, grabs the dog and runs through the door to freedom.

Plan your action sequence here

Ideas for action sequences

a penguin stampede, escaping from a prison, being chased by a dinosaur, a duel with a wizard, hiding from an alien, a sinking ship, swimming with piranhas, climbing a slippery cliff

Turn the page to continue...

Write a script for the action sequence you planned on the previous page.

All is quiet...

Uh oh...

Oh no!

Big impact

For every action sequence ask yourself: "How can I make this as exciting as possible?" A car chase down an erupting volcano will be more exciting than one on a quiet road.

Eeek!

Bad to worse

Think: "What's the worst thing that could happen?" Make that the thing that happens next.

AAAAAARGHHH!

terror
charge
BURST
smash
crush
leap
hurl
sneak
ALERT
hunt
wobble
grab
desperate
risky
awkward
impossible
deadly

Big bang
Give your action sequence
a dramatic ending.

Make 'em laugh

Telling a joke isn't the only way to make people laugh. Comedy writers have lots of tricks to make audiences chuckle, giggle and groan.

Exaggerate

One way to make a character funny is to find an ordinary FLAW and then EXAGGERATE it so much that it becomes ridiculous.

Create your own exaggerated characters below.

clumsy short-tempered forgetful proud

CHARACTER	FLAW	EXAGGERATION
Marcel	Vain	Always checking his hair in the mirror, even in the middle of an emergency.

Be mean but not nasty

Although it sounds unkind, audiences often find mishaps and bad luck funny. Pick one of the characters above and think of a few unlucky or embarrassing things that might happen because of his or her flaw.

Big disappointment

Another way to introduce comedy is to DISAPPOINT your character. Many comedies are about characters who try very hard to achieve their goals, but always end up disappointed.

> I really want to impress my new boss with a GREAT outfit.

> I'm so late! But I just don't have anything to wear.

> Maybe this will do the trick?

BUS STOP

> NOOOO!

A character has a goal. He makes a plan to achieve it.

The character tries to put the plan into action, but his flaws get in the way.

At the last moment, the plan is THWARTED and the character is disappointed.

Here are some examples of goals your character might have – add your own in the empty boxes.

Baking a cake	**Winning a competition**	....
Being on time	....	....
....	....	....

Now use the space on the two following pages to write a script about how your character tries and fails to achieve one of these goals.

HA HA HA HA HA HA HA

Be surprising

Audiences often laugh when they're taken by surprise. To come up with ideas, ask yourself what you'd LEAST expect to happen in the scene. What if a giant rubber duck appears, or everyone simply starts singing.

HA HA HA HA

Stay home?

Often, comedies are set in ordinary places such as family homes or schools. The contrast between an everyday setting and absurd events can be really funny.

HA HA HA HA HA HA HA HA HA HA

Big laugh

If your character suffers a series of accidents, make sure you save the most embarrassing mishap for the end of the scene.

Does your character succeed in the end?

A puppet show

If you're writing a script for puppets, you can breathe life into your characters by injecting them with BIG personalities.

Most puppets can't change their facial expressions, so it makes sense if they have ONE way of behaving.

They could be...

Snooty

Shy

Lazy

Evil

Clever

Kind

Grumpy

When you're creating a puppet character, you should pick ONE personality trait and blow it UP.

EVERYTHING your puppet says or does should reflect this character trait.

Add your own examples in the spaces below.

That's my motto

One way to help an audience recognize your puppet's personality trait is to give it a CATCHPHRASE – a short motto it often repeats.

Here are some examples of catchphrases. Can you think up one of your own?

I told you so!

Better luck next time!

DREAM ON!

Are we nearly there yet?

Hey-ho-let's GO!

You don't need proper puppets to put on a puppet show – nearly anything can be a puppet.

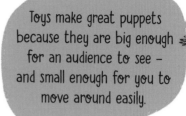

Toys make great puppets because they are big enough for an audience to see – and small enough for you to move around easily.

Personality clash

It can be exciting for audiences to watch characters with big personalities collide with each other. Write a scene about two puppet characters who argue over who should get the last cupcake in a bakery.

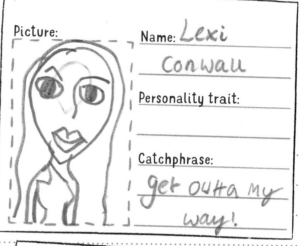

Picture:

Name: Lexi Conwall

Personality trait:

Catchphrase: get outta my way!

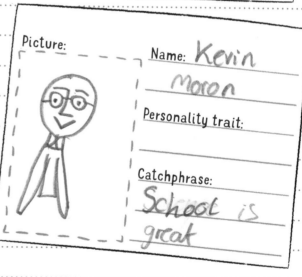

Picture:

Name: Kevin Moron

Personality trait:

Catchphrase: School is great

Turn the page to continue...

Get physical

Like cartoon characters, puppets can carry on performing, whatever happens to them.

This makes puppets great for physical comedy – they can do all kinds of crazy stunts. You can make them hang upside down, leap off tall buildings or even lose parts of their bodies...

The End

Boo!

Scary stories work really well as scripts – they're fun to perform and thrilling for audiences to watch. If you want to write a scary story, you'll need a combination of three ingredients.

1) A scary feeling

Everyone is frightened of different things... Some people are terrified by snakes or spiders. Some are scared of heights. Others can't stand the dark.

The first step to scaring other people is to think about what scares YOU. Write down three of your greatest fears.

1. Spiders
2. getting shouted at
3. being alone inday fire.

2) A scary situation

Pick one of the fears you've listed and imagine a situation in which a character might be forced to face that fear.

....
....
....

Someone scared of snakes might be visiting a zoo when suddenly all the cages open and the animals ESCAPE...

To make your situation even scarier, think about something else that will make things EVEN WORSE.

....
....
....
....

What if the zoo turns out to be HAUNTED?

Perhaps your character is TRAPPED in some way?

3) An UNscary character

The main character in a scary story is often extremely LIKEABLE. If audiences care about what happens to him or her, they're more likely to find the story scary.

You can make your characters likeable by giving them friendly names such as MR. CUDDLES or POLLY PUDDLEFOOT. Write your own examples here.

Now write down THREE appealing character traits that won't require much explanation, such as a silly laugh or a wacky dress sense.

1.
2.
3.

Use these three ingredients to write your own scary script.

You can create a feeling of DREAD from the beginning by suggesting a creepy SETTING.

Empty basement

Dark woods

Cemetery

Old ruins

Turn the page to continue...

Include creepy SOUND EFFECTS and PROPS to give your audience an extra fright.

Model spiders and snakes

Slime

Creaking

Fake blood

KNOCKING

Footsteps

Rustling

Rattling

Broken toys

Space out the scares

Leave short breaks between your scariest moments to give them more impact. That way you can also take your audience by surprise.

Perhaps your main character has a lucky escape and starts to feel safe. Then, when everyone least expects it, someone (or something) can JUMP OUT from the shadows.

Unfinished business

You don't have to tie up all the loose ends at the end of your story – if something is left unresolved, it will unsettle your audience and the scary feeling will last longer...

Dramatic conflict

All stories need conflict, moments where characters face challenges or obstacles. This keeps audiences gripped. It doesn't just mean filling your script with fights. With the right kind of conflict, a trip to the circus can be as dramatic as any battle...

Characters can face three main kinds of conflict:

Conflict with self

Conflict with others

Conflict with the setting

Here are examples of the three different types of conflict. Underneath there's space for you to create some conflicts of your own.

Self

a child with magic powers who wants to keep them secret

a chef with no sense of smell

a student choosing between homework and playing computer games

Others

rival spaceships race around the moon

a chess match against a champion

a bully at school

Setting

a steep cliff that has to be climbed

a tornado roaring closer

a tree a kitten is stuck in

If you want to make a scene really dramatic try introducing multiple types of conflict at the same time. Here are three problems facing Bingo, a trainee clown.

Self

Bingo wants to be a clown, but he isn't funny at all.

Others

His ringmaster boss bullies him all the time.

Setting

An escaped lion has wandered into the circus and is about to pounce.

Can you create another character from Bingo's circus facing different conflicts? It could be the lion, the ringmaster or someone completely new.

Character:

Self:

Others:

Setting:

Turn the page to continue...

Now write a script for a scene involving a series of conflicts. Choose Bingo, or the character you came up with on the previous page as your hero.

Conflict doesn't have to be about fighting

Your characters can struggle fiercely with each other without even raising their voices, let alone their fists!

It's time to start wrapping things up.
By the end of your script, try to
resolve at least one of the conflicts.

Teamwork

Most scripts are written BEFORE they're performed, but if you work in a small group, you can also do it in REVERSE. By working as a team, you can make something up as you perform, and then write it down LATER.

When performers make things up as they go along it's known as IMPROVISING.

I'm an ALIEN.

It helps if you decide on a few basic details before you start...

What if we were ALIEN HUNTERS?

Before you start improvising you should decide on a character, a setting and a situation. You can pick one from each of these columns, or add your own ideas in the lines below.

Who?

a naughty child

a strict teacher

a brave astronaut

a zany millionaire

Where?

a beach

a garden

a mountain top

a dark cave

What?

flying a kite

putting up a tent

riding a camel

having a party

Each performer needs to think about his or her character. Normally performers can learn about characters by reading a script, but when you improvise, you have to make it up yourself.

You can use the character questionnaire on pages 12-13 to help you.

Here are some suggestions that will help your performance flow naturally.

Make mistakes

The best way to improvise is to try out LOTS of different ideas. Many won't work – but you might discover something amazing.

Don't worry if you make a mistake – or you notice someone else has – simply carry on as if nothing has happened.

It's time to set off!

Y-y-es... off we go!

Pay attention

Watch the other actors carefully and notice everything they say and do. This will help you keep track of what's going on in the story.

She's amazing!

Say "Yes, and..."

Build on other people's suggestions – don't respond negatively to your fellow performers. Say "Yes, and..." to add your own twist to other people's ideas.

Let's hide from the alien under these blankets.

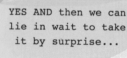

YES AND then we can lie in wait to take it by surprise...

Now you're ready to start IMPROVISING! Set a timer for ten minutes and see where the story takes you...

The next step is to REVIEW what you've just performed.

Which parts worked well?	Which parts didn't work?	How could they be improved?
....	....	....
....	....	....
....	....	....
....	....	....
....	....	....
....	....	....

Turn the page to continue...

You can use the parts that worked well to plan a story with a beginning, a middle and an end. If you're not sure how to do this, try giving your characters a problem to solve.

Problem

....

Beginning (discovering the problem)

....

Middle (experiencing the problem)

....

End (solving the problem)

....

You don't need to write everything out when you're improvising – you just need a few rough notes.

Your script only needs to mention key information.

Improvised performances are often unpolished. Performers stop and start, talk over each other and mix up their words. This can make these shows feel more natural and realistic.

The purpose of your script isn't to tell performers exactly what to say or do – it's to help them remember KEY EVENTS of the story.

You can help the performers stay on track by suggesting certain SIGNALS for them to make at fixed points, when it's time to move on with the story.

Once you've planned the story, try performing it from start to finish. After you've run through it, add more detail to the grid on the next page. This will become your script.

Beginning

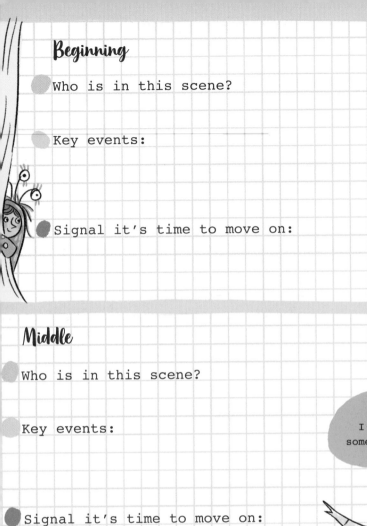

- Who is in this scene?

- Key events:

- Signal it's time to move on:

Middle

- Who is in this scene?

- Key events:

I think I just heard something QUACK!

- Signal it's time to move on:

End

- Who is in this scene?

- Key events:

- Signal it's time to end:

Signals

Here are some signals you could use to show it's time to move on – or you can think of your own:

- Do something – this could be as simple as WALKING OFF STAGE or as wacky as HOPPING WHILE SNORTING THROUGH YOUR NOSE.

- Say a code word when you're performing that the other actors will recognize. Pick an unusual word such as QUACK, PEANUTS or DISCO.

- Pick a key event in your story – maybe a character finds something that will be important later, such as a MAP, a MAGICAL CHARM or a SECRET DOOR.

In the dark

Now it's time to write an audio drama script. Think of it as a play performed in the dark – the audience can HEAR, but they can't SEE. You can help the audience picture the scene with a combination of WORDS and SOUNDS.

Think about the images you'd like to create for an audio drama about two friends on a camping trip.

Words

Every word your characters say will help to paint a picture.

Did you see that tree outside?

The clouds are covering the moon.

The more precise your words, the clearer the picture you paint.

Did you see that TWISTED OLD OAK tree outside?

The...clouds are covering the .... moon.

Sounds

Sound effects can bring your script to life. They help you tell the story and set the mood.

What might you hear on a camping trip? Can you add anything to these suggestions?

DOGS BARKING

Tent flapping

Footsteps thudding

Zipping

Twigs snapping

Animal snuffling

Sleeping bag rustling

Trees creaking

A strange noise wakes up the two friends in the middle of the night.
Will they be able to recognize it right away? What does it sound like?

....

....

....

It's pitch black. The friends look for a light but they can't find one...

Write a scene about what the friends do next –
don't forget to include sound effects in your script.

....

....

....

....

....

....

....

....

....

....

....

....

....

Turn the page to continue...

The sound of silence

Another tool you can use when you're writing an audio drama is to leave a pause between each character's speeches. Silence can have a powerful effect on your listeners. The exact effect depends on the length of each pause.

A **short** pause can sound like someone has just had an idea.

A **m e d i u m** pause can sound like someone's feeling embarrassed or uncertain.

A **l o n g** pause can create a sense of TENSION as the audience waits to find out what will happen.

Recording the audio drama

If you decide to record this script, you can create two very different settings to help your audience imagine the scene.

Try recording the parts of your script that are set OUTSIDE the tent somewhere that's really outside. You'll be able to hear a difference in the performers' voices and you might catch other sounds, like the wind blowing.

Sounds INSIDE the tent would be muffled. You can create this effect by building a pillow "fort" and recording these parts of your script here.

ZZZIIPP

Thinking aloud

People are thinking all the time, but they don't always say what's on their minds. So how can a script writer show what someone is thinking or feeling?

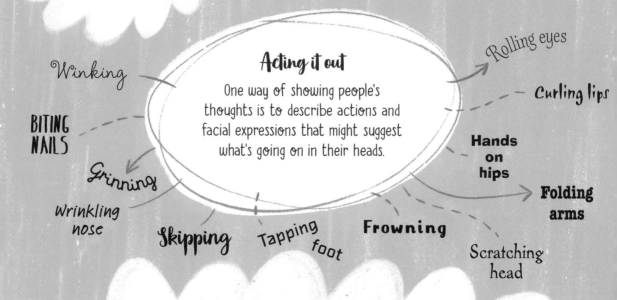

Acting it out

One way of showing people's thoughts is to describe actions and facial expressions that might suggest what's going on in their heads.

Winking

Rolling eyes

Curling lips

BITING NAILS

Hands on hips

Grinning

Folding arms

Wrinkling nose

Skipping

Tapping foot

Frowning

Scratching head

Stage whispers

Characters who speak in a stage whisper are only *pretending* to whisper – they're actually speaking loudly so the audience can hear them. This makes it seem as though the whispering character is sharing his or her private thoughts.

If you want your character to speak in a stage whisper, you can write it like this:

```
CHRIS: That cake looks tasty! Is it OK to try a slice?
(Stage whispers) I've had two already!

ABDUL: Of course! I'm so pleased you like it!
(Stage whispers) Fiddlesticks! I wanted it for myself.
```

Stage whispers are a handy (and often funny) way of showing that people don't always SAY what they MEAN. They tend to work best as short comments so they don't interrupt the flow of conversation.

There are many reasons why people don't say what they're thinking. Here are some examples:

Tom says he's not hungry when someone offers him food he doesn't like.

Nisha says she's finished her chores so she can go out to play.

Ying doesn't like her friend's new coat, but she says she thinks it looks good.

Describe another example of when a person might want to keep a thought to himself or herself.

Now imagine a character who is trying to keep this thought a secret. Can you think of any actions or facial expressions that might give your character away?

Write a script about someone who tries to keep a secret from someone else. Use actions, facial expressions and stage whispers to show what your character is thinking.

Turn the page to continue...

Breaking the fourth wall

Stage whispers can be an example of when
a character talks directly to the audience.
This is known as BREAKING THE FOURTH WALL
because it destroys an imaginary barrier
that usually separates performers from
the audience – the other three walls
are the sides of the stage or set.

Now imagine your character has been left alone and is wondering if it's wise to reveal the secret. Write these thoughts as a speech for your character to say out loud.

People often talk to themselves in real life, and they can do it in scripts, too. If this happens, it gives the illusion that the character is simply speaking his or her thoughts.

This trick is especially useful if a character has a difficult decision to make.

Try dividing this speech into three parts...

1 Why the character WANTS to reveal the secret.

2 Why the character DOESN'T WANT to reveal it.

3 What does he or she DECIDE? Why?

A war of words

Arguments make fun, dramatic scenes. How people argue is a great way to reveal what they are really like. Here are some tips for writing a good quarrel.

Each character should have a different argument style. Here the daughter is shouting, while the mother is calm, but cruel.

Often no words are said at all. People can argue through their actions too. But actions can lie...

This scene shows that the mother is selfish and manipulative and the daughter is hot-headed and needs love.

Here are a couple of ideas for argumentative scenes with space to add some ideas for scenes of your own.

Subject of argument	Arguer 1 and argument style	Arguer 2 and argument style	Setting
Bob and Clara disagree about what is the best kind of cheese.	Bob likes Cheddar. He gets very angry.	Clara likes blue cheese. She is calm.	a desert island
Rashida accuses Olaf of stealing, but Olaf says it wasn't him.	Rashida, a lawyer, is serious.	Olaf, actually guilty, is rude.	a courtroom

We're about to crash! Stop talking about lunch!

Not until you agree that lettuce is disgusting!

Clashing with setting

An argument is often more entertaining when it seems at odds with the setting. For example, a silly argument in a serious setting, or a serious argument in a silly setting can be very funny.

Choose one of the argument scenes that you came up with, and write it up over the following pages.

....

....

....

....

....

....

....

....

....

....

....

....

....

....

....

....

....

....

....

....

....

....

....

....

Ups and downs

One-sided arguments make boring scenes, so make sure both characters seem to be winning at different points as the scene plays out.

Fighting words

Take that back!

I can't believe you...

How could you...

Why did you...

How dare you...

What did you just say?

What is wrong with you?

You don't mean that.

You're just wrong.

Back off!

Are you talking to me?

Prove it!

Turn the page to continue...

How will you end your argument? Does somebody win?

The End

Going long

Often scripts are made up of lots of short scenes linked together to tell a longer story. Now that you've had some practice at writing short scenes, why not try GOING LONG? Here are some tips to help you plan a longer script.

1. The magic formula

Most stories fit into a simple three-part pattern.

Beginning

Introduce the setting and your hero.

Your hero has a desire or need but there's a big problem.

Middle

The longest part of your story. Your hero overcomes obstacles, and pursues his or her desire.

End

Story reaches climax.

Usually, the hero has to learn something new or change in order to succeed.

2. Timing

Think carefully about how long your script is going to take to act out. You also need to pace your story. Often, this means leaving enough time so your ending doesn't feel too rushed. A handy rule of thumb is that...

End — 1/4 of the story

Beginning — 1/4 of the story

Middle — 1/2 the story

3. Shapes for scenes

It also helps to think of each SCENE as a mini-story with its own beginning, middle and end. Remember that each time you change time or location, it's a new scene.

Beginning

Who's in the scene? Where are they? What is their goal?

Middle

Something changes. For example, if a scene starts happy, it should end sad.

End

Leave an unanswered question that leads to the next scene and moves the story forward.

Script plan

Here's an example of a script plan.

Title: The perfect cheese

Setting: Mountain farm

Main character(s): Sven and Nina

Character's goal: To make the perfect cheese

SCENE 1: We meet Sven and his sister Nina, dairy farmers.
A naughty cow has escaped. They chase it down. Good team.

SCENE 2: At home, a postman delivers a letter — an invitation to
a cheese-making tournament.

SCENE 3: Nina and Sven argue about cheese (traditional-style
v. science) — they resolve to compete against each other.

SCENE 1: Sven starts his cheese-making process. Traditional,
using his father's recipe. He can't get it right.

SCENE 2: Nina has disappeared. Sven continues to try to make
perfect cheese. Each batch something goes wrong.

SCENE 3: Days pass, finally, Sven brews up perfect batch.
But naughty cow kicks over mixture! Sven chases cow.

SCENE 4: Chasing cow, Sven finds Nina's secret cheese-making cave.
Ultra scientific. He allows cow to smash it up.

SCENE 5: Nina discovers what he has done. She is furious.
They fight. She runs away.

SCENE 6: Sven is distraught. He tries to mend Nina's stuff —
but it's all broken. Then he has an idea.

SCENE 1: After a long hunt, Sven finds Nina. He takes her home.
He has remade her lab using old-fashioned tools.

SCENE 2: Working together, Sven and Nina make cheese using
their combined techniques. Stressful! Must be perfect.

SCENE 3: Announcement of winner of tournament. Sven and Nina
are declared joint winners! Their cheese is perfect!

Turn the page to continue...

Plan your own script

Here's a blank form for you to use to plan your own longer script. If you want to plan more scripts, you can download extra forms from the Usborne Quicklinks website.

Title: ....

Setting: ....

Main character(s): ....

Character's goal: ....

Beginning

SCENE 1: _____

_____

_____

_____

SCENE 2: _____

_____

_____

_____

SCENE 3: _____

_____

_____

_____

Middle

SCENE 1: _____

_____

_____

_____

SCENE 2: _____

_____

_____

SCENE 3: _____

_____

_____

_____

SCENE 4: _____

_____

_____

_____

SCENE 5: _____

_____

_____

_____

SCENE 6: _____

_____

_____

_____

SCENE 1: _____

_____

_____

_____

SCENE 2: _____

_____

_____

_____

SCENE 3: _____

_____

_____

_____

Middle

End

NEXT STEPS

Now you've written lots of different
scripts, you might want to try performing
one of them in front of an audience.
This section will help you to do that.

A team effort

Putting on a show is often a team effort because it involves several different tasks. If you have a small team, one person can do more than one of these jobs – or even all of them.

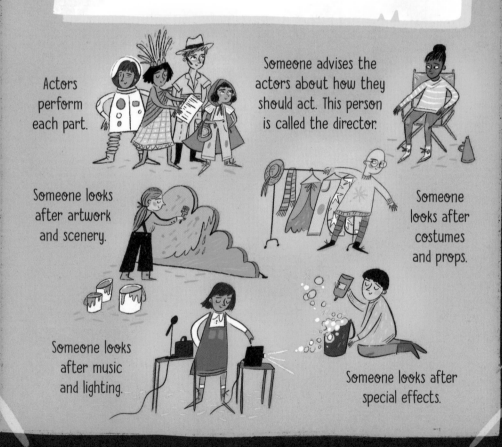

Actors perform each part.

Someone advises the actors about how they should act. This person is called the director.

Someone looks after artwork and scenery.

Someone looks after costumes and props.

Someone looks after music and lighting.

Someone looks after special effects.

Countdown to curtain-up

Putting on a show involves many different steps. This timeline will help you keep track of everything that needs to be done – and when.

 Decide who will do what – both behind the scenes and in front of an audience.

 Think about the character you're playing. Do you know any similar people? How do they behave?

 Sit together to read out the script all the way without stopping.

Work in progress

You don't have to treat a script as a finished piece of work – you can make changes to it as you rehearse.

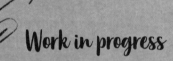

How am I going to learn all these lines?

Cut it down to make it shorter.

I hardly have anything to say...

Make changes to the size of people's roles.

What if I FAINT when she rescues me?

Rewrite parts to make them more dramatic or exciting.

7 Start rehearsing the script. This is when you make decisions about actions, music and special effects.

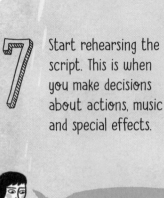

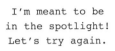
I'm meant to be in the spotlight! Let's try again.

I'll start playing the music after you walk away.

6 Performers learn their lines and actions by heart.

5 Rehearse the script without looking at it.

4 Prepare scenery, costumes and props for the performers.

The trick to putting on a great show is to rehearse lots of times, so you're as confident and well-prepared as possible.

I don't know about you, but I feel ready for ANYTHING.

3 Actors rehearse in costume and everything is done as it would be in a real performance – including music, lighting and special effects.

2 Lay out seats for the audience and prepare refreshments.

1 Now you're ready for the performance!

When you rehearse in costume, it's known as the DRESS REHEARSAL.

Inspiration board

You could use a scrapbook or a pinboard to note down ideas that inspire you.

5 classic movies I want to watch

THE RED BALLOON (1956)
A beautiful story about a little boy and a red balloon.

THE KID (1921)
Charlie Chaplin plays a poor man who rescues an orphan.

IT'S A WONDERFUL LIFE (1946)
George Bailey is shown what the world would be like if he hadn't lived.

BICYCLE THIEVES (1948)
A poor man searches Rome for his stolen bicycle.

SOME LIKE IT HOT (1959)
Two male musicians hide from gangsters by pretending to be women in an all-girl band.

Local DRAMA Nights!

If you want to get involved with live drama, try joining a local acting group. Local groups put on plays you can watch in your area too.

COOL SHOT

You can make sketches or cut out pictures of images that you really like from magazines. These can inspire stories, settings, shots and costumes for all kinds of shows.

Beak made with rolled paper

CROW COSTUME

Cape

UNDER SEA CAR IDEA

Be a critic ★★★★★

Write a review of a TV show you've watched.

Title: ....

....

Quick story summary: ....

....

....

What did you like about it? ....

....

....

....

What was the best scene? ....

....

....

....

What was the best line of dialogue? ....

....

....

....

How do you rate it? ....

....

....

/10

4 great cartoons

MY NEIGHBOR TOTORO (1988)
Two girls meet the spirit of the forest.

THE IRON GIANT (1999)
A boy becomes friends with an enormous war machine.

RANGO (2011)
A story about a very imaginative lizard and the stories we make up about ourselves.

KUBO AND THE TWO STRINGS (2016)
A boy goes on a spooky and dangerous magical quest.

If you hear an interesting piece of dialogue on TV, in a play or in a movie, jot it down to use later in your own script.

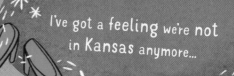
I've got a feeling we're not in Kansas anymore...

Making a movie

Here are some tips for turning your scripts into movies.
To start, you will need some actors and a camera or smartphone.

The three basic shots

Usually, movies are made up of brief filmed clips known as SHOTS. These are joined together later to make each scene. It's a good idea to use a variety of different shots in your movie.

Wide shot

Medium shot

Close-up shot

WIDE SHOTS film the action from far away. These are useful to show the audience where the scene is set.

MEDIUM SHOTS are used for conversations. They allow you to show a character's body-language and expressions. These are the shots that are used most often.

Filling the screen with an actor's face is called a CLOSE-UP. These can be very powerful, but be careful not to use them too often.

Take it again

You can film the same scene lots of times. That way, if an actor makes a mistake it doesn't matter. You might also experiment with different shots to see what works best.

That's not my cow!

Let's try that as a wide shot.

That's not my cow!

TAKE: 158

Moving the camera

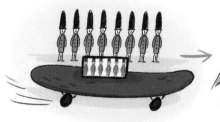

When you turn the camera from one subject to another as you are filming, it's called a PAN.

When the camera moves smoothly on wheels to follow the action, it's called a TRACKING SHOT.

To give the impression you are looking through a character's eyes, you can follow the action with a HANDHELD SHOT.

Editing your film

To put your film together, or "edit" it, you will need software on a computer or an app on a phone. Most work in the same way. You upload your shots to the app, pick the ones you like best and arrange them to make your film. Here are some editing tricks you can use.

It's a good idea to CUT unnecessary pauses in conversations.

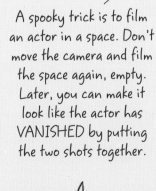

When you jump from one shot of something to another shot of the same thing it is known as a JUMP CUT. You can show time passing really quickly this way.

A spooky trick is to film an actor in a space. Don't move the camera and film the space again, empty. Later, you can make it look like the actor has VANISHED by putting the two shots together.

The edit is also where you add music and sound effects to your film.

CLOP
CLOP

Storyboards

Before starting filming, many filmmakers make a STORYBOARD. This is a series of sketches – a little like a comic book – that help you to plan out the shots you are going to use to film each scene.

Here's a storyboard for a scene in a school. Dialogue or a sound effect is added underneath each picture. You don't have to draw a picture for every line of dialogue – just the moments when the shot changes.

The pictures can be simple – just stickmen will do.

Over the shoulder shots like this are useful for filming dialogue.

TEACHER: Oxygen is a gas.

Sound effect: snoring

Try a close-up shot of a dramatic expression.

TEACHER: Carbon dioxide is a gas.

TEACHER: Argon is a gas.

KID: Huh?

Sound effect: ZOOM

On the opposite page is a blank storyboard for you to start planning how to film one of your own scenes. You can download more sheets like this from the Usborne Quicklinks website, or draw out your own on blank paper.

Sights and sounds

Putting on a show isn't just about reading out the words in a script – you can create a whole world for an audience using sights and sounds. These are some of the ways you might do that.

Scenery

Curtains can be used to mark the edge of the stage. They also control what the audience can – and can't – see.

Paint pieces of cardboard or paper to create background scenes. You can stick several small pieces together to make one really big piece.

If parts of the stage are at different heights, characters can be made to appear big and STRONG...

...or weak and vulnerable.

Scenery doesn't always have to be realistic – it's just a way of showing the audience where a scene is taking place.

Music

Music can set the mood. It can also signal to the audience when something is about to happen.

This is a fun song. It's so cheerful!

Shhh it's stopped! I wonder what's coming next...

Uh oh, it's that creepy tune again... I've got a bad feeling about this.

Lights and special effects

Always ask a grown-up for help with music and lighting – anything that uses electricity needs to be handled with care.

Lights are a good way of showing audiences WHERE to look. Spotlights help to focus their attention on one area.

Lighting can also set the mood – or show the audience what time of day it is.

Flashing a light and making a loud crash can create the effect of lightning.

It was a dark and stormy night...

A fan can be used to create the effect of wind.

Spray a window with a watering can, to create the effect of rain.

Costumes

An audience can tell a lot about what sort of character someone is from his or her costume.

Face paints or masks can help you change appearance.

Costumes are especially useful for stories set in the past.

You can use face paints to give performers exaggerated expressions so the audience can see them from a distance.

91

Set design and staging

A set is the stage or background where your script is acted out. A good set helps to tell the story too.

Be practical. You might find it tricky to set a convincing scene on the surface of the moon. It might be easier to build the interior of a spaceship with pieces of cardboard painted silver.

Details matter. A banana skin sitting on the floor willl create tension as your audience waits for someone to step on it.

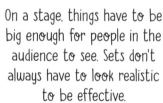

On a stage, things have to be big enough for people in the audience to see. Sets don't always have to look realistic to be effective.

Changing background details is a great way to show time passing from scene to scene. You can change seasons by adding falling leaves, or snow. Even just adding dirty dishes to a table can be an effective way to show that a few hours have passed.

In the spaces below, sketch two set designs for two scenes that you've written.
You can download more sheets like this from the Usborne Quicklinks website.

Putting on a show

When you are ready, you can perform your play, or show your film in front of your friends and family. Here are some finishing touches for your show.

Design a poster

An eye-catching poster will make people excited to see your show.

Use one strong image to give an idea of what your show is about.

Make sure people know where and when it starts.

DOOM CAW

in the living room
Saturday, 2pm

DOOM CAW
Saturday, 2pm
Seat: Pink comfy armchair

Tickets

Even if your show is free, it's a good idea to give out tickets. They make great souvenirs for your friends and family.

Create an atmosphere

You might want to decorate the stage and have music playing before your show starts. This will put your audience in the right mood for your story.

Take a seat

There are lots of different ways to arrange seats around a stage.
The most important thing is that everyone in the audience has a good view.

Take a break

Longer shows have breaks in the middle
called intervals or intermissions. You might
use the break to serve refreshments.

Take a bow

At the end of the show, it's traditional for
the actors to line up and bow to the audience.
This is to say "thank you" to the audience for their applause.

Invite everyone who helped with your show onto the stage at the end.
That's a great way to thank them for their work.

95

Acknowledgements

Writing tips by Andy Prentice and Matthew Oldham
Illustrated by Hannah Peck
Designed by Laura Wood and Tabitha Blore
Edited by Ruth Brocklehurst

Photographs

page 9 Wooden spoon | © Oleksandr Shpak | Dreamstime.com
page 9 Eiffel Tower statue | © Tony Bosse | Dreamstime.com
Additional photography by Laura Wood

Every effort has been made to trace and acknowledge ownership of copyright.
If any rights have been omitted, the publishers offer their sincere apologies
and will rectify this in subsequent editions following notification.

The websites recommended at Usborne Quicklinks are regularly reviewed but Usborne
Publishing is not responsible and does not accept liability for the availability or
content of any website other than its own, or for any exposure to harmful,
offensive or inaccurate material which may appear on the Web. Usborne Publishing
will have no liability for any damage or loss caused by viruses that may be
downloaded as a result of browsing the sites it recommends.